# WISDOM
## on Faith

## RICHARD C. HALVERSON

VISION™
HOUSE
PUBLISHING, INC.
*Gresham, Oregon 97030*

WISDOM ON FAITH
© 1995 by Richard C. Halverson

Published by Vision House Publishing, Inc.

Edited by Chip MacGregor
Cover Design by Multnomah Graphics
Interior Design by Martin Bogan

Printed in the United States of America

*International Standard Book Number:* 1-885305-18-4

*Vision House Publishing, Inc.*
*1217 N.E. Burnside Road, Suite 403*
*Gresham, Oregon 97030*

Scripture references are from:
New American Standard Bible, The Lockman Foundation © 1960, 1962, 1963, 1968, 1971, 1972, 1973, 1975, 1977. Used by permission.
New International Version, © 1973, 1978, 1984 by International Bible Society. Used by permission of Zondervan Publishing House.
All rights reserved. The "NIV" and "New International Version" trademarks are registered in the United States Patent and Trademark Office by International Bible Society. Use of either trademark requires the permission of International Bible Society.
Revised Standard Version of the Bible, © 1946, 1952, 1971, 1973, Division of Christian Education, National Council of Churches of Christ in the USA. Used by permission.
J. B. Phillips: The New Testament in Modern English, J. B. Phillips © 1958. Used by permission of Macmillan Publishing Co., Inc.
The Good News Bible in Today's English Version, © 1983. Used by permission of Thomas Nelson, Inc.

95 96 97 98 99 00 01 02 03 04 — 10 9 8 7 6 5 4 3 2 1

# 1

**H**ow does one think of faith?

Do not think of it as *buying power* — as "coin of the realm" — as a means of exchange of which one has more or less to purchase smaller or larger blessings.

Do not think of faith as a *virtue which merits a reward* from God...

Like a father giving his child a piece of candy for "being a good boy."

Do not think of faith *quantitatively* — as though it came in pints and quarts... in ounces and pounds.

Think of faith *qualitatively*...

Like *openness to a person:* You are introduced to a stranger — you hold out your hand — take His — "receive" Him at face value.

Think of faith as *responding to a person* (or any other fact) affirmatively — as opposed to rejection.

Think of faith as *acceptance of that person*...

Beginning a *personal relationship* which can be nurtured and developed into a deep friendship.

Think of faith as an *accepting — growing — deepening relationship with Jesus Christ.*

The Lord Jesus Christ *makes Himself known* through the Bible — through His disciples — in worship.

A personal relationship with Him is *nurtured by these same means.*

Like a stranger knocking at your front door waiting for you to open and invite Him in, *Jesus Christ stands at the door of each man's heart,* quietly knocking — patiently waiting — for acceptance.

"Behold I stand at the door and knock. If any man hears my voice and opens the door, I will come in unto him and sup with him and he with me."

*— Revelation 3:20*

**F**aith?

*Faith in what?*

It is what or who one believes in that causes faith to make sense!

The object of faith *determines the validity* of faith.

In what does your faith rest?

Does it rest in your faith? Do you have *faith only in your faith?* That's a meaningless cycle — like loving love.

Does your faith *rest in your intellect?* Your ability to reason? Your understanding? Your ability to think things through?

Is your head the *court of last resort?*

Does your faith rest in your *emotions* — your feelings?

Does your faith rest *in the dramatic* — the spectacular? *Do you always need something exciting* to happen in order to believe?

Or does your faith rest *in the Word and work* of Jesus Christ?

Do you need more than this for faith — *more than the integrity of Jesus Christ* — more than His promises?

If so — *you have something other than New Testament faith.*

Faith in *anything less than the sure Word of God* — the completed work of His Son Jesus Christ — is not the faith taught in the Bible.

Faith in man himself — however it expresses itself — is *doomed to disillusionment...* maybe even despair.

Faith in one's faith — or intellect — or emotions — or experience — is *inadequate faith* which will never support one in the crucible of life.

To live by faith — to walk by faith — is to trust — to rest — in the *faithfulness of God*, the *trustworthiness of Jesus Christ*, the sufficiency of His love and grace, the certainty of His promises.

"We walk by faith, not by sight."

— *II Corinthians 5:7*

"The righteous shall live by faith."

— *Romans 1:17*

# 3

**R**ecently a conversation with a commercial airline pilot reminded me of a *fundamental fact of faith...*

His description of *instrument flying* was very vivid — and relevant to faith.

As an instructor, when flying with a student, he often *induces vertigo* — then turns the controls over to the student.

Invariably the student's "feel" is *contrary to the instruments.*

He reacts wrongly... his strong tendency is to *believe his feelings* instead of his instruments.

The student must learn to operate *against his feelings* in obedience to the instruments.

If he doesn't *he will destroy himself!*

*Faith works that way...*

Authentic faith *depends upon the Word of God* no matter how strong one's feelings may be to the contrary.

The Bible is to the believer *what the instrument panel is to the pilot.*

The basic discipline is to learn to *believe against feelings.*

Feelings are a *result of believing...* not a basis for believing.

Obeying the instruments, the pilot *goes through adverse weather* and lands safely at his destination...

Believing the promises of God one is taken through difficulties of every shape and size...

But he *arrives safely!*

" ... in all things God works for the good of those who love Him, who have been called according to His purpose... neither death nor life, neither angels nor demons, neither the present nor the future, nor any powers, neither height nor depth, nor anything else in all creation will be able to separate us from the love of God that is in Christ Jesus our Lord."

— *Romans 8:28, 38, 39*

# — 4 —

**F**aith is *believing what you cannot know*," the university student said.

That is *not an uncommon idea* of faith…

As though faith is a *second or third best way* of going.

Knowledge — by which is meant *intellectual apprehension* — is assumed to be the best way.

If one cannot know, then the next best thing is just to *believe anyway*…

The implication being that such a position is *at best precarious*.

"Do you trust so-and-so?" I asked — naming a friend with whom I know the student was unfamiliar.

"How can I trust him?" she asked. *"I don't even know him!"*

"But you said faith was believing what one cannot know," I reminded her. "Now you say you cannot trust someone you do not know — which is correct?"

The answer is obvious!

*One cannot have faith in what one does not know!*

*Faith begins with knowledge* — and rests upon the integrity of the thing or the one known.

*Without knowledge* there can be no faith!

They have *no knowledge* of the Bible — of God — of Jesus Christ... They are ignorant of the life-sustaining promises God has given in His Word...

Therefore they are *without faith.*

Faith is not something that can be generated within one by struggle or effort. *Faith comes with knowledge* of that which is trustworthy.

"Faith comes by hearing and hearing by the Word of God."

*— Romans 10:17*

**F**aith does not come *by struggle!*

Faith is *effortless…*

The *quiet response of a man's heart* to one who is trustworthy.

It is *deeper than an intellectual response.*

In fact — it is not uncommon to trust someone you do not completely understand.

Jesus' disciples *often did not understand Him…*

But *they trusted Him!*

His words at times were *incomprehensible…*

Nevertheless He *inspired confidence.*

Except in those who *would not accept* Him.

Not that they could not… *they would not!*

*Thomas had some doubts* on occasion…

Jesus satisfied them so thoroughly that he could declare, "My Lord and

My God."

The man who says he cannot believe in Jesus Christ should examine himself — *ask himself if he is willing to believe.*

If he is willing but cannot — *Jesus will meet him in some faith-generating way* that will resolve his difficulty.

If he is unwilling, there is nothing Jesus — or anyone else — can do to convince him.

No man is convinced against his will.

Obviously *evidence is meaningless* to the man who refuses it.

"Yet to all who received Him, to those who believed in His name, He gave the right to become children of God."

*— John 1:12*

**D**o you have faith in God...

Or faith *in your ideas* about Him?

Is God *real...* or just an intellectual concept?

Is He *personal...* or academic?

Is He a *living reality* in your life... or just a theological proposition?

How big is your God?

Is He *limited to your understanding* — your intellectual grasp — your rational explanations?

*Your God is too small* if He is no larger than your ideas about Him!

You are, in fact, creating your god and he is no god at all, but an idol — a logical (more or less) syllogism, *the product of your own intellect.*

Which means that *you are bigger than your god* — as the creator is greater than his creature. You are the creator — your god is your creature...

No wonder you have no respect of God! No wonder you do not expect anything from Him! No wonder life is inside out and upside down. No wonder your *values are transposed* and you don't really know what you are living for!

No wonder your religion has form without power. *Half-hearted faith* is inevitable when men downgrade God to their size.

You're living in a spiritual vacuum — don't be surprised when life seems hollow. You've got a capital Zero where God ought to be! You're worshipping Nothing!

Want to get squared away? Get your eyes off yourself, your ingenuity, your intellectualism... take a long, clear, *honest look at Jesus Christ.* Ask Jesus to make Himself known to you. *He will make God real* to you... if you let Him!

"For although they knew God, they neither glorified Him as God nor gave thanks to Him, but their thinking became futile and their foolish hearts were darkened. Although they claimed to be wise, they became fools... "

— *Romans 1:21-22*

**F**ive weeks after my 20th birthday (February 4, 1936) a young man, who later became my first pastor, introduced me to the Bible, *which had been a closed book to me up to that time.*

More specifically, he introduced me to an *incredible promise* in the Bible, John 5:24. Jesus speaks: "Verily, verily, I say unto you, he that heareth my word, and believeth on him that sent me, hath everlasting life, and shall not come into condemnation; but is passed from death unto life."

"You have heard Jesus' word," the young man said, "do you believe?" *Of course I believed Jesus... I had no reason not to...* though I knew very little about Him at the time.

"Then, do you have everlasting life?" he asked. That threw me! He asked me to read the text and repeat it in my own words. "Jesus said that *if one hears his word and believes, he has everlasting life,*" I replied.

"Do you believe Jesus?" he asked again. Yes! "Then, if you believe Jesus, did He not say that you have everlasting life?" *That's what Jesus said!*

Suddenly, the light dawned... If I believed, I had everlasting life... If I did not have everlasting life, I did not believe... *it had to be one or the other!*

No flash of lightning — no thunder clap — no change in feeling (at least for two weeks) — but I believed Jesus' word, therefore, I must have everlasting life. Nor could I "come into condemnation," for I had "passed from death unto life."

For forty years I have lived in the light of that word of Jesus. *I put my faith in Him.* I have failed often — and sinned much — and, for a brief period in 1942, doubted that I really had everlasting life...

But in a time of self-despair, I was restored to full assurance — not by some spectacular experience, *but by returning to the simple recognition that by believing Jesus' word... I had everlasting life!*

Now past seventy-five, I can testify to the faithfulness of Jesus Christ. He has never failed — nor has His word. *I rest my future — my eternal welfare — solely upon His word!* It is a sure and solid foundation.

Again and again, through the years, I have put the *full weight of great personal need* down upon the Bible. Never have I been disappointed... *Never have I regretted putting my faith in Him.*

Jesus never fails!

F*aith in faith* is nothing…

     *Faith in God is everything!*

Faith without God is illusion…

     It is *God who validates* faith.

Faith does not save…

     *Christ saves!*

Faith does not heal…

     *Christ heals!*

Faith does not change human nature…

     *Christ changes human nature!*

Faith is not a *cause*…

     Faith is an *effect!*

Faith is not humanly generated...

        Faith is a *gift of God!*

Faith in faith is *futile*...

        Faith in God is *triumphant*...

Not because of faith...

        But *because of God!*

"For it is by grace you have been saved through faith, and that (faith) not of yourselves, it is the gift of God."

— *Ephesians 2:8*

# — 9 —

**F**aith in God and man are *inseparable!*

Think right about God — *you'll think right about man...*

Inevitably!

The two are indivisible — *one's view of God determines one's view of man.*

Which is the hidden peril in atheism... it inescapably *downgrades human nature...*

A reality which is not so obvious where atheism is *protected by a culture rooted in Judeo-Christian values...* but very apparent where atheism is policy...

As, for example, *human rights* in Marxist countries.

Communism failed because communism *violates human rights with contempt* as it is founded on atheism.

Such is the foundation for secular humanism. An optimistic view of man which denies his sin is a *false optimism*, doomed to disillusionment.

True optimism in man is based, not in faith in his perfectibility — but *in faith in God's love for him.*

Marxism is not just a political system — it is a way of life — *a total view of life and history* — which rejects God and, hence, rejects man. Humans are important only as they serve the cause.

Marxism promised a new social order and *it was a matter of indifference how many humans were destroyed in the process.*

Your faith in God reveals your value of mankind.

High view of God — *high view of man.*

Low view of God — *man loses his value!*

"So God created man in his own image, in the image of God He created him; male and female He created them."

*— Genesis 1:27*

**K**arl Barth, Swiss theologian, said, "Religion is infidelity because it is man's faith in himself." Christianity is *faith in God*.

The confusion of Christianity with religion is one of the *false equations* of the twentieth century.

Actually, on the basis of a point by point analysis, *Christianity and religion are at opposite poles*. They are not only unlike each other — they are in direct and complete opposition.

In religion the emphasis in on man. *Religion is man-centered*. Man is the subject — God is the object. Man is the doer — God is the One done for. Man is the giver — God is the receiver.

Perfect statement of religion is the shallow cliché which came out of pre-World War II days: "Man is the measure of things."

Christianity is the antithesis! *In Christianity God is central*. God is the subject — man is the object. God is the doer — man is the one done for. God is the giver — man is the recipient.

The perfect statement of this is "God so loved the world that He gave His only Son, that whoever believes in Him shall not perish but have eternal life."

*— John 3:16*

*Religion is faith in human nature* — the belief that man is able by his own effort — his own works — his own ethical and moral achievements — to please God and attain righteousness.

Christianity is faith in Jesus Christ. His death and resurrection. Human nature being basically sinful is helpless to please God. *Man is a sinner and needs a Savior.* Jesus Christ is that Savior! He saves by the power of regenerating human nature.

Religion aims at the *refinement of human nature* by whatever method.

Christianity aims at the *regeneration of human nature* producing a new creature — a community of changed men. Your faith in God is unique!

Religion is man seeking God — Christianity is God seeking man.

Religion is man's attempt to discover God by the unaided intellect. Christianity is *God's revelation of Himself* to man — to any man who will let God be known to him.

The apostle Paul puts it this way: "We are His workmanship, created in Christ Jesus to do good works, which God prepared in advance for us to do."

*— Ephesians 2:10*

**F**aith that is sure of itself is not faith... Faith that is sure of God is the only faith there is."

So wrote Oswald Chambers in *My Utmost for His Highest* for December 21. *He states a profound and practical truth.*

There are two kinds of reality: objective and subjective.

There is reality in *facts outside* one's experience — and there is *reality within* one's personal experience.

Amazing how philosophers and psychologists have argued about this... *trying to eliminate one or the other...* and this controversy does not escape Christians.

There are those who think of faith as purely subjective: the only reality is their experience.

Their theology — if they have any — is based upon their experience. *They argue from subjective experience* — the final proof for everything is their experience.

They insist that others share *their* experience... coerce if necessary, that others may... then withdraw from them if they refuse or are unable to have the same experience.

Unfortunately, *such faith is at the mercy of feelings and emotions.* When they are absent — faith languishes and is often abandoned in disenchantment or worse.

*Authentic faith* is never sure of itself... it *is only sure of God!* It rests upon the *objective reality of certain historical facts:* the Bible, Israel, Jesus Christ, the apostles.

Authentic Christian experience is a *result* of which believing the objective facts is the cause!

Experience is a delightful confirmation of the truth of the objective reality — *but the facts are true* whether one experiences something or not.

If I believe the Bible, God's Word written... and Jesus Christ, God's Word incarnate... *what the word says is true...* whether or not my faith is accompanied by a subjective experience.

Forgiveness of sin — spiritual regeneration — new life — God's love and acceptance — peace — *are all mine when I believe the Word!*

"This is the work of God, that you believe."

*—John 6:29*

# ~~ 12 ~~

**W**e walk by faith — *not by sight...*

That's plain enough!

We walk... *not by sight...*

If words mean anything — we live in violation of that biblical principle *if we depend upon the visible.*

We so easily become the victims of the visible.

How many professed followers of Christ — for example — suffer chronic frustration and guilt *because they do not see results* from their witness...

At least results *like others profess* to have.

Despite the clear word of Jesus — "He who abides in me and I in him, he it is that bears much fruit — for apart from me you can do nothing."

*— John 15:5*

On the *authority of His word* — we know we are fruitful when we abide in Him and His word abides in us.

In our lust for results — we turn it around and *make fruit the test for abiding...* if we bear fruit we are abiding.

How do I know I'm bearing fruit? *Because I can see it? Not if I walk by faith!*

I know I'm bearing fruit if I abide in Him — *because He said so!*

If results are the basis for my faith — *I'm not trusting Jesus' word!* I'm not walking by faith!

Put the *focus on abiding in Him...* fruit is inevitable.

"We walk by faith, not by sight."

— *2 Corinthians 5:7*

**O**minous days and threatening circumstances hold no fear for the man of faith… they afford him opportunity to *demonstrate the stuff* of which his faith consists.

Faith is idle when circumstances are right — *only when they are adverse* is one's faith in God exercised.

Faith, like muscle, *grows strong and supple with exercise.* Soft living leaves it flaccid.

As alternate firing and cooling temper steel to the required hardness and toughness — *difficulties strengthen character.*

The man who has been tried in the fire is not brittle — does not crack under the strain!

Christian character is *not automatic*… it involves a process which is often painful and unpleasant.

Patience, for example, comes through tribulation. Pray for patience, God will likely *answer with trials.*

Humility, the queen of virtues, comes *only through humiliation.*

Even the Son of God Himself, we are told, "learned obedience through the things which He suffered."

In His providence, *God knows* how much joy and sorrow, how much pleasure and pain, how much prosperity and poverty is proper for His child. He knows the correct balance of sunshine and storm, the *precise mixture* of darkness and light it takes to perfect a son.

The faith of our fathers is "living still in spite of dungeon, fire and sword."

Their faith, and ours, lives still because it is *utterly adequate* for the blackest day — the fiercest storm.

In times like these the authentic Christian is invincible!

His faith is in the Lord of history — the unchanging God who "works in everything for good to them that love Him."

" ... I will fear no evil, for Thou art with me."

*— Psalm 23:4*

**F**ear not, stand still, and see the salvation of the Lord."

*— Exodus 14:13*

Hardly good advice *under the circumstances...*

Israel at the *Red Sea — mountains* on one side — *desert* on the other...

And the *Egyptian army pursuing fiercely* in great force.

Some probably rejected Moses' counsel as *unrealistic — if not worse.*

*Some panicked* — ran into the sea and drowned...

Or up into the mountains or out in the desert and *perished.*

Only *those who stood still* were safe. *Only those who had faith in God!*

All God had to do was *open a path through the Red Sea...*

But *who is his right mind* would ever have expected that?

We have a penchant for *limiting God's actions to a few alternatives* that we can think up under pressure...

And assume that our paltry options *exhaust all possibilities.*

Inaction *when action is clear* is a cop out...

But doing anything *just to be doing something* is worse!

Action for its own sake may leave *irreparable damage* or lead to bad *direction which is irreversible.*

When one does not know what to do... *doing nothing is something!*

Waiting on God is the *wisest strategy.* Have faith in Him.

*No time is lost* when one waits to act until he is sure God is leading.

"He that believeth shall not make haste."

*— Isaiah 28:16*

I t takes *great faith* to be an atheist!

It is *inaccurate* to say that the atheist does not believe in God…

An atheist *believes in No-god!*

*That takes a lot of faith!*

Because the *weight of evidence* is to the contrary.

Believing in No-god is *holding a faith against overwhelming evidence…*

*Universal evidence…*

Evidence *within man* himself — his conscience.

Evidence in *history…*

Evidence in *nature…*

No to mention the multiplied evidence of *millions in every generation* who have taken the Bible seriously…

Who have tested God's promises and *found them to be true*...

Who have enjoyed a *personal* — *first-hand experience* of the living Christ.

To believe in No-god is to hold a faith against *hundreds of thousands of volumes* written by thousands and thousands of authors over thousands of years...

All of which witnesses to *a personal God who has made Himself known* to all who would receive the truth.

Atheism is irrational...

Which is why the Bible says, "The *fool* has said in his heart there is no God."

— *Psalms 14:1*

"In the beginning God... "

— *Genesis 1:1*

**G**od has a plan for your life!

That is the *exciting prospect* for your future!

God desires to lead you in that "good and acceptable and perfect" way which He has had planned for you *before you were conceived* (Psalm 139:13-18).

He will not impose it upon you — *He will not coerce you.*

He has given each of us the *freedom… and the responsibility* to choose His plan… or to reject it. He will not *violate our personal sovereignty.*

Paul declares that we were "made by Christ" — and we were made for Christ. By Christ… *for* Christ!

To be Christ's is our ultimate destiny!

But we are His only *as we give ourselves to Him.*

We can be ourselves only as we are *possessed by Christ*… only as we have faith in Him and *accept His rule* in our lives.

Do you have the faith to accept God's wonderful plan for your life?

In the National Gallery of Art hang some of the great originals — done by the artist himself — his own oils — his own strokes... *and they are masterpieces!*

In a little shop at the gallery, one can purchase *copies of the originals* for a dollar...

Each of us must decide whether he will have faith in God, give himself to Jesus Christ and *become the divine original* He intends...

Or whether we will refuse Christ... and *remain a cheap copy of what we might have been.* It is a matter of faith.

*The choice is yours!*

"I urge you, brothers, in view of God's mercy, to offer your bodies as living sacrifices, holy and pleasing to God — this is your spiritual act of worship. Do no conform any longer to the pattern of this world, but be transformed by the renewing of your mind. Then you will be able to test and approve what God's will is — His good, pleasing and perfect will."

— *Romans 12:1-2*

od *knows* you...

God *loves* you...

God *cares* for you...

God *desires the very best for you!*

Can you have faith in a God like that?

He is *not surprised by your sin and failure* — in fact, He knows your weaknesses better than you do yourself.

And He has provided an *infinitely adequate remedy* in the person of His Son...

Who *lived* for you...

*Died* for you...

*Rose again* from the dead for you!

Can you have faith in a God like that?

God has given His Holy Spirit to *indwell you* — to live the life of God in you — to *produce the life of Christ in you*…

To *empower* you to be what you ought to be…

What you *desire* to be.

Can you have faith in a God like that?

A God who offers all the resources you need for life here and now — and in the eternal future.

God has *given us His Son!*

"In Him are hidden all the treasures of wisdom and knowledge."

*— Colossians 2:3*

"For God was pleased to have all His fullness dwell in Him."

*— Colossians 1:19*

"Christ in you, the hope of glory."

*— Colossians 1:27*

# — 18 —

The *keeping power* of God!

It is fundamental to understanding the *supreme security* the believer enjoys in Jesus Christ.

Faith in the biblical sense is *not holding on to God*…

It is realizing that *God holds on to you*.

Illustrated by a *father's walk with his child*…

As they go *the child holds on* to the father's hand…

The child stumbles — falls — his *little grasp unable to hold on* to his father's big hand.

This happens a few times and finally the *father grasps the child's hand* in his.

Again the child stumbles — but he does not fall…

The *father is holding on* now.

Eternal salvation is *the work of God* from first to last.

*It does not depend upon our holding on* — or keeping up — or following through.

If it did, eternal salvation would be meaningless — because it would be *dependent upon human effort.*

Eternal salvation is *God's idea* — *desired by God for all* humanity — free to any who accept it — receive it.

It is wholly, completely, *totally dependent upon God's faithfulness and love.*

"For it is by grace you have been saved, through faith — and this not from yourselves, it is the gift of God- not by works, so that no one can boast."

*— Ephesians 2:8-9*

"Now to him who is able to keep you from falling and to present you before his glorious presence without fault and with great joy... "

*— Jude 24*

**F**aith is *not wishful thinking.*

Faith is *not a leap in the dark.*

Faith is *not believing what you cannot know.*

Faith alone is nothing — a cipher.

*Faith in faith is a zero!*

Add zeros to zeros and *you still get nothing…* no matter how many zeros are added.

But put an integer in front and *nothing equals something…*

The integer makes the difference…

God is the integer of faith.

Faith (which is nothing in itself) in God *equals everything!*

His integrity — His dependability — His trustworthiness — His faithfulness *makes faith reasonable.*

*It is God who gives faith value.*

To trust Him only for what He does for you is not to trust Him at all...

Waiting to see results before we trust Christ *is to trust results... not Christ.* To trust Christ is to trust Him *no matter how contrary your feelings or circumstances.*

He is *infinitely faithful* — that's what causes faith to make sense.

He is *worthy to be trusted!*

Faith in a God *who cannot fail* will not fail.

*God makes the difference.*

As one put it, "What we need is not *great faith* in God — but faith in a great God."

"Yet he did not waver through unbelief regarding the promise of God, but was strengthened in his faith and gave glory to God, being fully persuaded that God had power to do what he had promised."

— *Romans 4:20-21*

od is God!"

That definition of God comes from one of the clearest — the most brilliant intellects among theologians of the twentieth century — Karl Barth.

Can you think of a more simple definition... or more profound?

Or do you feel it is *no definition at all*... just tautology?

Try this then...

Finish this sentence: God is like...

_____

How would you *fill in the blank?*

How does your faith picture God? *What is He like?* What do you believe *He can do?* Who do you believe *He is?*

Much theology messes it up. No word or words can be added — no analogy — that *does not diminish God.*

God met Moses on Mt. Sinai and *gave him his mandate* — emancipate Israel my people!

"Who shall I say hath sent me" inquired Moses.

"I am that I am — tell them that I AM hath sent thee."

Can you *improve upon that?*

*God is God!*

"To whom, then will you compare God? What image will you compare him to?... He sits enthroned above the circle of the earth, and its people are like grasshoppers. He stretches out the heavens like a canopy, and spreads them out like a tent to live in. He brings princes to naught and reduces the rulers of this world to nothing... Do you not know? Have you not heard? The Lord is the everlasting God, the Creator of the ends of the earth. He will not grow tired or weary, and his understanding no one can fathom. He gives strength to the weary and increases the power of the weak."

— *Isaiah 40:18, 22-23, 28-29*

**E**ither God *is*... or God *is not!*

If God is not — then *nothing matters* anyway...

Humanity will go on doing the best that it can in its fantastic scientific and technological progress — *perennially victimized* by its own selfishness — failure — and sin.

With all his progress — man keeps *refining the instruments of his own destruction*.

But *if God is*...

Then *there is hope* — even for sinful, hedonistic, selfish mankind...

*He loves* — *He cares* — nothing is too hard or impossible for Him!

If God is... *either He is in charge of history or He is not.*

If He is not — *mankind is without hope* — his aspirations are illusions — life is irrational and absurd.

But the Bible records the exciting fact that *God is in charge of history.*

As someone has said, *"History is His story."*

History is going somewhere — *it has a purpose* — a consummation!

Life has *meaning!* Man has a *destiny!*

*Put your faith in God!*

"He made known to us the mystery of His will according to His good pleasure, which he purposed in Christ, to be put into effect when the times will have reached their fulfillment, to bring all things in heaven and on earth together under one head, even Christ."

— *Ephesians 1:9-10*

"We know that in everything God works for good with those who love Him, who are called according to His purpose."

— *Romans 8:28*

od desires to and delights in *directing your life!*

Nothing is clearer in the Bible than the *guarantee of Divine guidance* to anyone who seeks it.

Every day of your life can be *God-planned and directed!*

*Day by day...*

*Moment by moment...*

*Step by step...*

God *has* led — that is the *testimony of history.*

As one *looks back over his life* in retrospect, one can see how beautifully — wonderfully — lovingly God has led.

"I praise the Lord, the God of my master, who has led me on the right road," testified the servant of Abraham.

God *will* lead — that is the testimony of doctrine.

The Scriptures *teach it by precept and example* throughout the Old and New Testaments.

Academically it is relatively easy to believe that God will lead in the future. The Word of God declares it to be so. Looking ahead — *before one needs direction* — before the crunch — one can testify the Lord *will* lead.

God is leading! That's where the "rubber meets the road."

That is the *testimony of faith!*

God has promised to lead... I seek to be led... that's an *unbeatable combination* — God's promise, my submission.

God *has* led — for which I am grateful. I know He *will* lead — and for this I praise and thank Him.

God *is* leading! This is my confidence and joy... my rest!

"Trust in the Lord with all your heart and lead not on your own understanding. In all your ways acknowledge Him and He will direct your paths."

— *Proverbs 3:5-6*

Choice! The unique gift of Creator God to the crowning glory of creation — humans.

Freedom to choose — *to believe God or to disbelieve God.* To love or to ignore Him. To serve God or to reject Him.

The sovereign God Himself will *never interfere in this matter.* He instructs — He commands — but He *never forecloses* on the freedom He guaranteed in His original creation.

But, in His infinite wisdom He ordained that *choice determines destiny!* Choice has consequences!

Our first parents exercised this freedom. God had spoken — Satan also spoke — and in so doing *directly contradicted God's Word.*

Incredibly, they *chose to believe Satan's lie* — rejected God's Word in disobedience. And in their *self-alienation* — their unbelief of God — they determined *the destiny of humanity.*

All alienation in history *derives from their original choice.* Alienation — war — became the *consequence of that choice!*

Whether between husband and wife, parent and child, management and labor, neighbors, races or nations… *No power in human history has been able to remove those consequences!*

Government, be it dictatorship or democracy, has failed. Education has failed. Law has failed. *Even the perfect Law of God* (Romans 8:4).

But God was not without remedy. He sent His Son who lived, taught, sacrificed His life on a cross — rose from the dead to provide *a way of escape from the awful consequences of wrong choice.*

Which provides *another choice* each is free to make — to put your faith in God's Son or not. To accept Him or reject Him. In His infinite love, God does everything in His power to induce us to choose His Son… but *He will not force or coerce.* Each is free to choose or to reject His Son.

But there are consequences! To choose Jesus Christ is the way of redemption — eternal life — salvation… To reject is *the way of judgment* — condemnation — eternal damnation.

"For God so loved the world that He gave his only Son, that whoever believes in Him should not perish but have everlasting life."

— *John 3:16*

# — 24 —

The man who *knows where he is going* is greatly admired in our culture. He is to be *emulated*.

The one who is *sure of himself* — who has "all his ducks in a row" — is considered an *exemplary model* in 20th century America.

The one who has *defined his goals* — planned the strategy by which to achieve them — whose P.E.R.T. chart conforms to the plan — honored.

In our *evangelical subculture*, this is the way we tend to think — this is the kind of person we want most to be like.

Is it conceivable that this is "worldliness" — secularism — materialism — in the *most subtle and seductive sense?*

Consider Abraham — *giant of the faith* — *father of the faithful* — whose "seed" was to bless "... all the families of the earth... "

"... He went out, not knowing where he was to go."

*— Hebrews 11:8*

"... He sojourned in the land of promise, as in a foreign land, living in tents."

*— Hebrews 11:9*

He was *a nomad — a desert wanderer* — as were "... Isaac and Jacob, heirs with him of the same promise."

*— Hebrews 11:9*

Abraham "... looked forward to a city which hath foundations, whose builder and maker is God."

*— Hebrews 11:10*

*His hope lay beyond history.* He was the father of our faith — no better model as we look forward to a new century.

"For my thoughts are not your thoughts, neither are your ways my ways, saith the Lord. For as the heavens are higher than the earth, so are my ways higher than your ways, and my thoughts than your thoughts."

*— Isaiah 55:8-9*

**T**o wait on God is *not to do nothing!*

It is *not an excuse for apathy* or negligence...

It is not to *sit on one's hands* and watch the world go by.

To wait on God is to believe Him when He says He will "direct our paths."

To wait on God is to *seek His direction* — His light — His way.

To wait on God is to *be sensitive to the indwelling Holy Spirit* who delights in leading us in the Father's will and way.

It is to *listen for the "still small voice"* of I Kings 19:11-12.

To wait on God is to be *totally involved in the process* of God's leading — to be involved effective and efficiently...

Not to wait on God is to *waste time and energy*... and foul up the process.

Not to wait on God is to *risk acting precipitously and prematurely.*

The one who waits on God is *not in a hurry* — does not panic — practices patience — enjoys the peace of God.

To wait on God is to *wait on the divine initiative* — to respond in harmony with God's plan and purpose for one's life.

One *never waits too long* — no time is ever lost — for God promises to lead "step by step" — moment by moment.

"He that believeth shall not make haste."

*— Isaiah 28:16*

Allow your faith to wait on the Lord.

"They that wait upon the Lord shall renew their strength."

*— Isaiah 40:31*

## 26

**W**hen the situation is hopeless…

*That's the time for faith!*

Actually there is *no such thing as a hopeless situation* for one who trusts in God…

But the fact is that most of us turn to God *only when we think the situation is hopeless!*

As long as we can find something in our circumstances on which to pin our hope *we trust that possibility* rather than God.

*Until we have used up all our options* — see no shred of hope in our circumstances…

Then — *as a last resort* — we may turn to God.

Someone put it this way: "As long as we have reason for hope, we hope in the reason."

As long as we can think up possible answers — *we depend upon human ingenuity* — or luck — or coincidence...

Then, when alternatives are exhausted and there is nowhere else to turn...

We *give God His chance.*

In other words, *we only think we are trusting God* when circumstances are favorable... we are actually trusting circumstances.

How much better to *trust God no matter what!*

"In hope Abraham believed against hope... No distrust made him waver concerning the promise of God."

*— Romans 4:18, 20*

**H**ave you ever tried to play a stringed instrument when the strings are loose?

*Tension is essential to melody!*

And it is *essential to life!*

Of course you can tighten the strings of an instrument *too tight*…

In which case — if you don't break them — *you'll get discord.*

But *the solution is not loose strings.*

The solution is *proper tension.*

Tension is *essential to faith* also.

There is *much about God that we cannot understand*… much about the Bible and Jesus Christ that is a mystery…

How could it be otherwise — with a finite creature attempting to know the infinite Creator?

Like trying to get the ocean in a tea cup.

In the pursuit of the knowledge of God *truth often seems contradictory* — tension results.

The one who insists on relieving the tension eliminating one side of the paradox *comes up with a half truth.*

*God's sovereignty* and *man's freedom* for example...

How can both be true?

Rather than accept the tension, some *reject one side of the other...* and fail to comprehend the God-man relationship.

They've solved their dilemma... but either *they get so up tight* with their half view that they are close to breaking...

Or they quit trying to think at all — *resign to an attitude of indifference* and neutrality.

*The music goes out of their lives...* just deadness is left.

"The righteous live by faith."

*— Romans 1:17*

hat does it mean to *"walk by faith?"*

How does one "walk by faith?"

First — *it is to walk "not by sight."*

Does this then mean that one *walks blindly?*

No more than the pilot of a 747 flies blind when he is being *talked into a landing* by the control tower.

No more than when a pilot *believes his instruments* when they disagree with his "feelings."

One of the hard lessons a pilot learns is to *trust what you know to be true* when it disagrees with what you "feel."

He is in *much greater danger* by depending on his feeling than by depending on his instruments.

Ceiling zero — visibility zero — very poor conditions to fly by sight…

But the aircraft lands safely when the pilot *listens to the word* from the control tower and obeys it.

To walk by faith is to *heed the word of God*…

To *read* it — to *know* it — to *learn* it — to *obey* it.

It isn't those who walk by faith that *louse up their lives*…

It is *those who walk by sight!*

Jesus said, "I am the light of the world, he that follows me shall not walk in darkness but shall have the light of life."

*— John 8:12*

**S**anctification... *a much misunderstood word.*

Some think of it as "perfection" — whatever that means — or to be *sinless* or *otherworldly* or *pious* or *unreal*... some think of it as *self-improvement.*

But one does not need God for self-improvement... many who have no interest whatever in the Holy Spirit take self-improvement seriously.

Our whole culture — godless or godly — is conditioned to self-improvement...

Many, if not most, expend a good deal of time, effort and money to improve themselves... with little, if any, interest in spiritual matters.

Sanctification is a process... spiritual maturation... it is to grow more and more into the likeness of *Jesus Christ.*

That is not to say one is to imitate Jesus Christ — which is impossible — (how does one imitate God) — *but it is to recognize that Christ indwells the believer* and His inward life is allowed to manifest itself more and more outwardly.

One *learns to depend upon himself less and less* (the very opposite of self-improvement) — and grow in his dependence upon Christ within.

In the process one learns from failure and sin which spring from human weakness — *his inability* to live Christ-like — together with the *supreme adequacy of Christ* within.

In other words one is learning the *meaning and power of grace* as one puts faith in God.

As grace "reigns" within — the believer *grows in his hatred of sin and in his love of righteousness.*

He *trusts self less and less... Christ more and more!*

"... in order that the just requirement of the law might be fulfilled in us, who walk not according to the flesh but according to the Spirit."

— *Romans 8:4*

## 30

**T**he crunch in the walk of faith is not in the *area of responsibility*...

It is in the area of *human pride*.

*Man his own god!*

That's *humanism* — the universal religion — born in the garden of Eden.

By whatever name it is *man's faith in himself* — not God.

*Despite the record of human failure* individually and collectively throughout history...

Man *refuses to admit his need* — his sin — his dependence upon Almighty God.

Humanism is the belief that in one way or another *humanity is its own Savior.*

The corollary to humanism is the position, expressed or unexpressed, that the *Bible is wrong* — Jesus Christ was wrong — the apostles were wrong...

The *bodily resurrection* of Jesus Christ is a fraud...

The *crucifixion of Jesus Christ* was a waste...

Paul and Peter and the other apostles were *false witnesses*.

The fact is the more one trusts Christ *the more sensitive one is to his responsibility* to God and to others...

And the *more effectively responsive* to it.

Authentic faith in Christ simply *does not beget irresponsibility!*

On the contrary — the one who believes that God is fully in charge of history — whose God is big enough to handle the macrocosm as well as the microcosm — who *takes the Lordship of Christ seriously*...

Is of all people the one most concerned *that he fulfill his obligations in life.*

He is most *desirous of conforming to his Lord's will* — and to respond obediently to his responsibility whatever the situation in which he finds himself.

"Faith without works is dead."

*— James 2:17*

## 31

How do you measure life? Like you measure a string, by its length? Methuselah lived more than 900 years... *which is all we know of him.* Some of our best were taken by war before they were 25. Some of the greatest died young. *Life is more than length!*

Do you measure life by breadth — sphere of influence? Alexander conquered the whole world and cursed his childhood *because he never learned self-control.*

Hitler controlled more of the modern world than any other single man. Who wants to emulate Hitler? *Life is more than breadth.*

Do you measure life by its height? Popularity — wealth — fame? Many have *reached the top and discovered emptiness.* They made it — but were never sure what "it" was.

Real greatness is measured in depth. Everything else about a tree depends on its roots — everything else about a building depends on its foundation. *Depth is the measure of the person!*

Shallow people can't take pressure... are good only for fair weather... scatter like buckshot in a crisis.

One with depth is like the sea... winds of circumstance may ruffle the surface — *underneath are great, quiet, untroubled depths.* With depth, one stands in the critical hour.

Such persons meet the real emergencies. They're with it when great thinking, strong leadership, or decisiveness is necessary.

The *deep life, the mature soul is not an accident.* It is the product of time for relationships with God — Scripture — prayer — spouse — children... Too busy for God or others is to be too busy!

"They that wait upon the Lord shall renew their strength, they shall mount up with wings as eagles; they shall run and not be weary, they shall walk and not faint."

*— Isaiah 40:31*

## 32

**V**acant." *What an epitaph for a tombstone!*

A long-time friend had a very serious auto accident which involved long-term recovery.

Contemplating his death — a real possibility for awhile — he told his wife he wanted *one word on his grave…*

*"Vacant!"*

Which would have been *precisely accurate* — for one who has faith in the Lord Jesus Christ.

If he had died, *he would not have occupied the grave.* His body would — but not he!

"Absent from the body, present with the Lord," declared the apostle Paul in II Corinthians 5:8.

Jesus said, "I am the resurrection and the life… He that lives and believes in me shall never die."

*— John 11:25*

He also said, "I go to prepare a place for you… and if I go to prepare a place, I will come again and receive you unto myself that where I am there you may be also."

*— John 14:2-3*

The Psalmist wrote, "Though I walk through the valley of the shadow of death I will fear no evil, for Thou art with me."

*— Psalm 23:4*

Paul declared, "For me to live is Christ — to die is gain."

*— Philippians 1:21*

That's the biblical view of death. *It is to gain.* It is to *be with Christ.*

Death is not the end for the one who has faith in Christ… it is a *grand beginning* — to be fully alive.

The body — once inhabited by the one who goes to be with Christ — is placed in the grave *there to await the resurrection* of the body which will occur when Christ re-enters history to consummate His redemptive purpose.

"I… desire to depart and to be with Christ, which is far better."

*— Philippians 1:23*

# 33

**D**o you believe God… or just your beliefs about Him?

Here's the difference between what one has called "bumptious security" and authentic *Christian assurance*.

Nobody is surer than a fanatic!

He's absolutely, unshakably convinced in what he believes. In fact, that's precisely what makes him a fanatic. *His views are final!*

He's so convinced in his beliefs that he has stopped thinking.

At best, he just rearranges his prejudices.

The true Christian *believes God*…

Even though he is not sure of God's ways — because God "works in mysterious ways his wonders to perform" and God is therefore unpredictable.

Fanaticism is predictable, and because it is, the one who is so limited finds life to be *increasing monotony and boredom.*

*Righteousness is unpredictable.* This does not mean that it is erratic — righteousness is absolutely consistent, trustworthy, and logical — but by Divine, not human, standards.

The true Christian is certain of God — though *uncertain of what God will do next...*

But absolutely certain that whatever God does is right, perfectly right.

For this reason, therefore, the authentic Christian life is an adventure filled with thrilling expectancy — *expectancy in God and His righteous overrule of life.*

The Christian may not know the way — but he *knows the One Who is ordering his steps.*

He does not know what to expect, but he does know that whatever it is, it will "work out for good to those who love God, who are called according to His purpose."

He knows that life is a risk — but he has risked his life with God!

"If God be for us — who can be against us?"

— *Romans 8:31*

One of the most common errors in the thinking of those who profess faith in Christ is the idea that *faith is meritorious* — that it has value in and of itself...

Like *purchasing power* with God.

Faith is thought of *as a means of getting what one wants* from God. If one just has enough faith he gets his answer.

Faith is a *quantitative commodity* — one has more or less faith... the more he has, the greater his buying power with God.

Such thinking leads to *frustration* — *or worse*... guilt.

As in the case of those who *blame themselves for the death of a loved one.* "If we had *just had enough faith*, he would have lived." Or, "If we just had enough faith, he would be healed."

Thinking this way — *how much is enough?*

Faith ought to be thought of as the *means whereby one relates to God* — trusts in Him — has confidence in His wisdom, His integrity — His faithfulness — His utter dependability.

Faith in the biblical sense is to *believe God no matter what.* It is to trust God *whether feelings or circumstances encourage or support such confidence* or not.

In fact, true faith often has to choose to believe God against feelings — against circumstances — against everything that opposes faith.

Job had the right idea: "Though He slay me, yet will I trust Him."

*— Job 13:15*

Paul put it this way: "… Let God be true but every man a liar."

*— Romans 3:4*

Faith *holds fast to the fact* that "God works in everything for good to those who love Him."

*— Romans 8:28*

# — 35 —

The *growing edge* of the spiritual life is need!

Which is *absolutely contrary* to the way of our culture.

Our culture enthrones strength and power! *The powerful person is adulated* — advertised — admired... despite the awful lessons of history on the *destructive nature of power* in man.

*Nothing corrupts more than power* — nothing is more destructive of humanness...

It turns *lambs into lions... humility into arrogance.*

*God's way is the way of weakness!*

Human strength tends to *alienate from God...* weakness turns one to God.

It was the *strong and righteous* who rejected Jesus Christ — the weak and sinful found in Him *love, compassion and acceptance.*

Jesus said, "They that are strong do not need a physician... The Son of Man is come, not to call the righteous but sinners to repentance."

Putting your *faith in Christ* means denying *pride, power, and arrogance* — accepting the strength, wisdom, and healing of God.

*Human pride* finds this way of life abhorrent... *glories in human strength* — despises weakness.

God's ways are *the very opposite*...

"For my thoughts are not your thoughts, neither are your ways my ways, says the Lord. For as the heavens are higher than the earth, so are my ways higher than your ways, and my thoughts than your thoughts."

*— Isaiah 55:8-9*

"Blessed are they that hunger and thirst for righteousness, for they shall be filled."

*— Matthew 5:6*

"Without me you can do nothing."

*— John 15:5*

"And He said unto me, 'My grace is sufficient for you, for my strength is made perfect in weakness.' Therefore I will boast all the more gladly about my weaknesses, so that Christ's power may rest on me."

*— II Corinthians 12:9*

## 36

**I**t is not enough just to be against — or to be neutral...

What are you for?

If you refuse the way of Christ — *what are your alternatives?*

You will not believe in Christ...

In whom then will you believe?

You will not come to Christ...

To whom them will you go?

You will not follow Christ..

Whom then will you follow?

You will not put your faith in Christ...

In whom will you *put your faith?*

*You believe something* even if you insist that you don't believe in anything...

Believing in nothing is something!

*You are following someone* — even if you insist you are following nobody.

*You are living for something* — even if you're so busy making a living you do not know what you are living for.

*You are going somewhere* — even though you may be so completely preoccupied with the present that you ignore the future.

*You've got a destiny* — one way or the other — even though you are indifferent to it.

*What are the alternatives* if you will not have Christ — follow Christ — be Christ's — take Christ's way?

Honestly — do you know a better, more intelligent, more honorable and fulfilling way?

You're on your way... why not make it *the way?*

Jesus said, "I am the way, the truth, and the life; no one comes to the Father except through me."

— *John 14:6*

"He that is not with me is against me."

— *Matthew 12:30*

## 37

**B**orn again"… an often misunderstood — and sometimes maligned phrase.

But a good word — describing a *profound, but simple reality.*

Not just a *buzz word* from a fundamentalist subculture in the Bible belt…

But a *sound biblical truth* introduced by Jesus Christ Himself.

Birth has to do with *life.*

Genesis 2:7 records: "And the Lord God formed man of the dust of the ground, and breathed into his nostrils the breath of life; and man became a living soul."

"Breath" in Hebrew is the word for spirit. God put His Spirit — *the Spirit of Life* — into the first human.

Which is what *occurs in the new birth* — when one is born again.

The only difference is that the first man had no choice... ever since, *each of us is free to choose* — or reject new life.

When we choose, when we put our faith in God, He gives us His Spirit and *we become eternally alive!*

"But as many as received Him, to them He gave the power to become children of God — children born not of natural descent nor of human decision or a husband's will, but born of God."

*— John 1:12-13*

*Born again* — all those who have *put their faith in God!*

"In reply Jesus declared, 'I tell you the truth, unless a man is born again, he cannot see the kingdom of God... Unless a man is born of water and the Spirit, he cannot enter the kingdom of God. Flesh gives birth to flesh, but the Spirit gives birth to spirit.'"

*— John 3:3, 5-6*

## 38

**T**hey call it *universalism...*

The belief that *all will finally be saved* — that no one will perish because of sin.

In other words, there is *no fear of hell.*

Generally its final appeal is the justice of God — the implication that a just and loving God *would not ultimately reject anyone.*

Which is true...

*God will not — does not reject anyone!*

But the problem is not God's rejection of man — *it is man's rejection of God.*

God loves the world and *everyone in it* throughout history.

His love is *universal and all-inclusive...* a perfect love in which God sent His only begotten Son to die on the cross for all in every generation from the first to the last.

But God *cannot force* anyone to accept that love!

God will not *coerce faith* in His Son.

That would not be love — that is coercion which *denies the freedom God guaranteed to man in creation.*

Rejection of creation *repudiates that freedom.*

God created man free — *free even to reject God* — to reject His will — His order — His salvation... even His love.

Sin is *disbelief and rejection!*

To reject God's truth and God's love is *the profoundest of sins* — the fundamental sin of history.

*Salvation is universal...* Christ died for all — and *desires all to enjoy heaven.* But the stubborn fact is that *not all believe and accept His love* — His salvation. Many — perhaps most — reject it!

God has not rejected man — *they have rejected God!*

"This is the condemnation, that light is come into the world and men loved darkness rather than light because their deeds were evil."

*—John 3:19*

## 39

**A** landholder planted a vineyard — *let it out to tenants* — departed for a far country. In due time he sent an employee to collect his portion of the harvest. The tenants *beat the employee* — *sent him away empty-handed.* More employees were dispatched — *each received the same treatment.*

Finally the landholder sent his son, thinking, *"They will respect my son,* pay him our share of the harvest." But the tenants heaped the *final infamy* — *they killed his son!*

That parable of Jesus is the *story of history...* the *story of humanity...*

God set man in a *perfect world* with the command to *cultivate it and enjoy it.*

*Man's response was a rejection* — rejection of God's command in deference to a usurper... and subsequently through the centuries, man has *repudiated God's ownership of the world* which He created.

That is *sin in its fundamental essence!*

God has sent many servants into His prodigal world: deliverers, judges, prophets... and *finally His own Son.*

God's message was rejected — the prophets were stoned — and when the Son came... *they crucified Him!*

Humanity continues to crucify the Son of God. Not with a crown of thorns or spittle or ridicule.. but with *condescension* — patronage at best... or by utterly *ignoring Him* and *blaspheming His name* in careless profanity.

The Bible insists, "The earth is the Lord's and the fullness thereof, the world and those who dwell therein."

*— Psalm 24:1*

Jesus taught, "The cares of this world, the deceitfulness of riches and the lust for things choke the Word of God" in the hearts of men.

Humanity *rejects the Divine Proprietor* — ignores His prior claim — prides itself in ownership and acquisition — *idolizes possessions...* then wonders why compounding affluence generates destructive inflation — fragments society — and polarizes people and nations into the "haves" and the "have-nots."

"All the believers were one in heart and mind. No one claimed that any of his possessions was his own, but they shared everything they had. With great power the apostles continued to testify to the resurrection of the Lord Jesus, and much grace was upon them. There were no needy persons among them, for from time to time those who owned lands or houses sold them, brought the money from the sales and put it at the apostles' feet, and it was distributed to anyone as he had need."

*— Acts 4:32-35*

## 40

**D**ogma... or faith?

Which describes *your profession?*

There's a wide difference...

Dogma has to do with *the head*...

Faith has to do with *the heart.*

Dogma is *rational*...

Faith is *transcendent.*

Dogma is *belief in propositions*...

Faith is *trust in a person.*

Dogma *breeds intellectual pride*...

Faith breeds *humility.*

Not that dogma and faith are *mutually exclusive*... true faith involves dogma — doctrine — propositional truth...

But faith begins in a *relationship with the person Jesus Christ!*

Doctrine grows from this — but is *always less then the relationship* and must never be allowed to replace it.

The bottom line... do you simply believe your beliefs about Christ — or do you know Him — trust Him — love Him?

Is He the *essence of your faith* — or is it only your theology about Him?

"Now this is eternal life: that they may know You, the only true God, and Jesus Christ, whom You have sent."

*— John 17:3*

"The work of God is this: to believe in the one He has sent."

*— John 6:29*

## 41

It's not what happens *to you* that makes the difference...

It's what happens in you!

What happens to you is destructive *only in terms of what you allow to happen in you.*

To put it another way — you may not be able to prevent what is done to you... but *you can decide how you respond to it.*

You can decide what your attitude will be!

You may *allow circumstances to embitter you* — make you vindictive — jealous — envious...

But when you do you release emotions in your system which *trigger body chemistry and poison you.*

Or you may take circumstances in stride in the confidence that your life is ordered of the Lord and that *He will use everything that happens to you for your own good.*

*Growing in grace* and in the knowledge of Jesus Christ works this way...

*Your faith* grows this way.

The *school of the Spirit* involves suffering — pain — failure — sin...

All of which are *recycled by the grace of God* into maturity.

*Don't resent* what happens to you...

*Have faith in God and in His plan*...

*Rejoice* in the knowledge that God is working for your benefit in whatever happens.

"And we know that in all things God works for the good of those who love Him."

*— Romans 8:28*

## 42

**F**aith is not blind!

Faith *begins with knowledge.*

In and of itself faith is nothing — *it must have an object* — and knowledge of that object is basic to faith.

Would you cash the check of a *stranger without references* you knew?

Faith *depends upon knowledge* of that in which it rests.

Without that it is *powerless* — and *meaningless.*

Which explains the *disappointment* — even *disillusionment* — some have experienced.

They thought they had faith in God when actually *they only had faith in their faith* in God.

Or they had *faith in their doctrine* — or a *preacher* or teacher — but they did not really have faith in God.

*God alone is trustworthy and faithful!*

No matter how we feel — or what happens — *He is dependable!*

Faith is *not getting what I want* — or having things work out the way I planned them...

Faith is *not even dependent upon God fulfilling His promises!*

(Not that He cannot — but that He may not!)

Twice in the *greatest chapter on faith in the Bible* — Hebrews 11 — it is recorded: "... these all died in faith, not having received the promise."

To have faith in God is to *believe God no matter what happens!*

Which is why authentic faith praises God in difficulty and adversity — He is *worthy of praise* whatever the circumstances!

Whatever the facts — however adverse — *God is the supreme fact!*

"Faith comes by hearing and hearing by the Word of God."

Abraham was "not weak in faith when he considered his own body now dead... and the deadness of Sarah's womb... but was strong in faith, giving glory to God."

*— Romans 4:19-20*

# 43

**V**ictims of the visible...

*Believing only what is seen* — if that.

The *refusal to believe* what one cannot see.

The *perilous assumption* that nothing is happening simply because one does not see it happen or is uninformed.

The *presumption* that prevails when we act and talk as if the only thing God is doing is what is happening *where we are and in what we are doing.*

The humiliation felt when we learn of an amazing work of God *totally apart from anything we are doing* — without any connection, without work or any work of which we are knowledgeable.

If one must see to believe he needs to learn faith...

Faith which holds to an omniscient, omnipotent, omnipresent God Who is infinitely more concerned — more caring — more loving than we — *Who works when and where and how He pleases* — with or without human agency...

Faith in *a God who is faithful* to His own sovereign purpose...

Faith in *a God who does not fail* — for whom nothing is too hard...

Nothing impossible.

Faith in a *God who is not overwhelmed* by any circumstances — Who is not asleep — or on a holiday — or indifferent.

It may be error or sin *to believe that God is in something that He is not*...

But it is infinitely worse *to live as though God is not in something when He is!*

"The things which are seen are temporal. The things which are unseen are eternal."

*— II Corinthians 4:18*

## 44

**W**hat is God like?

What does your faith say He is?

How do you envision Him?

Is He *like a giant* with an intellect far greater than human intelligence?

Is He *like a great animal or bird?*

If there were no Bible, *where would one look* to find God?

Would one invent Him?... But *how does one invent the uninventable?*

How does one *imagine the unimaginable?*

If one could invent or create a god, *he would be greater than the god he produced.*

The Bible reveals a God who is *infinitely beyond human comprehension.*

He is *eternal*... He has no beginning, nor ending.

He is *omniscient* — Lord of history and Ruler of nations.

He *commanded the universe into existence.*

The Bible has a great deal to say about the gods *invented by humans*.

"Their idols are silver and gold, the work of men's hands. They have mouths but they cannot speak. They have eyes but they cannot see. They have ears but they cannot hear. They have noses but they cannot smell. They have hands but they cannot handle. They have feet but they cannot walk. Neither do they speak through their throats. They that make them are like them, so is everyone that trusts in them."

*— Psalm 115:4-8*

Praise God! *Our faith is in a personal God who loves us and is involved in our lives!*

## 45

**I** awoke early one morning in Vienna with this thought...

There is *only one enemy*...

God!

And the issue is *rarely drawn and resolved*...

Because we *refuse to acknowledge it.*

*Not that God is really an enemy...*

He is the *supreme friend!*

He *made us*...

He *loves us*...

He *died for us*...

He *desires us*...

But we will not yield — *we will not accept His love and reciprocate.*

We will not *put our faith in Him.*

We *make Him the enemy!*

And *religion* is often the weapon we use.

In the name of religion we spar with God — *keep Him at arms length* — sometimes slug it out with Him.

We do precisely what the Serpent in the garden *convinced our first mother, Eve, that she should do…*

"Eat that fruit and be like God."

She ate — but in so doing, she rejected God's word — disobeyed His command — *repudiated her God-likeness* which was His gift in creation…

And alienated herself — and us — from God.

Generation by generation we humans keep on doing it. *Striving to be perfect ourselves in our own wisdom and strength,* we reject God's reconciliation and perfection in Christ.

We *heed and obey the real enemy, Satan* — disbelieve and disobey the true Friend, God… and make Him the enemy.

"They exchanged the truth of God for a lie and worshiped and served the creature rather than the Creator."

— *Romans 1:25* ✚

## 46

**J**ust a simple set of metal shelves...

Four horizontal pieces of metal to be bolted to four vertical strips...

Included was simple plan of assembling.

As we struggled to put it together *we discovered that there was a right way*... if we did not follow the simple plan we were frustrated... the bolts would not go through.

*Life is like that!*

It was *made to work God's way!*

The Maker has given *clear instructions* which are contained in the Bible...

Which is, so to speak, the *operation manual* which comes from the factory.

*The instructions are simple* — just ten commandments!

God *wrote them on the human heart* when He created Adam and Eve.

They *express themselves through human conscience.*

When conscience is ignored or rejected *it is seared and silenced.* When it is seared and silenced, *inner restraint is removed...*

Sin is easy — even desirable... and *totally destructive!*

*The disintegration of our social order* can be simply explained.

Increasing crime, alcoholism, drug abuse, divorce, family instability, corruption in public life, poverty, inflation, armament races, etc., etc. etc. ...

All result from the fact that *we have disobeyed the clear instructions* of God concerning life. The *Bible has become a closed book.*

Friend in the faith, *open your Bible!*

"For the wages of sin is death, but the gift of God is eternal life through Jesus Christ our Lord."

— *Romans 6:23*

## 47

**T**he trouble is we're sick…

*Our whole nation is sick…*

Sick unto death!

And to make matters worse, the country is full of quacks pandering to medicine-man remedies.

Political remedies… economic remedies… social remedies… religious remedies…

*None of which touches the disease!* All of which *aggravate the agony!*

The is *only one Great Physician*… Jesus Christ.

There *only one adequate cure*… His cross and resurrection.

Name *any of the social diseases* that infect our world: war, prejudice, poverty, addiction, crime…

At the *roots of every one of them* is human sin — pride, greed, avarice, lust, laziness, selfishness, jealousy, envy, malice.

A condition *precisely diagnosed by Jesus:*

"What comes out of a man is what makes him unclean. For from within, out of men's hearts, come evil thoughts, sexual immorality, theft, murder, adultery, greed, malice, deceit, lewdness, envy, slander, arrogance and folly."

*— Mark 7:20-22*

The Gospel of Christ is *the only remedy* for that deadly malignancy!

*Faith in Jesus Christ* is the tonic for the sickness in the world.

Like any medicine *it must be taken* to work.

If it is rejected, *the disease will rage unchecked* to its violent, destructive consummation — despite the ingenious, innocuous poultices frantically applied by sophisticated, contemporary man in his lust for relevance.

Nor will it help simply to hold the gospel as a *cherished doctrinal position!* (Tragically, some who hold the gospel dearest *demonstrate its relevance least.*)

It must be taken — applied — submitted to — *obeyed!*

"I am not ashamed of the Gospel of Christ, for it is the power of God to salvation for everyone who believes; first to the Jew, then to the Gentile. For in the Gospel a righteousness from God is revealed."

*— Romans 1:16-17*

## 48

The way of the kingdom of God is *antithetical* to the way of our contemporary culture.

Our culture says, "Blessed are those who have it together — *who have made it.* Blessed are the achievers." Jesus says, "Blessed are the poor is spirit... "

Our culture says, "Blessed are those who *couldn't care less* — who are on top. Blessed are those who promote self." Jesus says, "Blessed are those who mourn... "

Our culture says, "Blessed are *the mighty* — the powerful. Blessed are those who flaunt it." Jesus says, "Blessed are the meek... "

Our culture says, "Blessed are those who are *not restrained by moral and ethical taboos.* Blessed are those who live it up." Jesus says, "Blessed are those who hunger and thirst after righteousness... "

Our culture says, "Blessed are the *manipulators* — the oppressors. Blessed are the influential." Jesus says, "Blessed are the merciful... "

Our culture says, "Blessed are those who, *if it feels good, do it!*" Jesus says, "Blessed are the pure in heart... "

Our culture says, "Blessed are the *strong* — the drivers. Blessed are the movers and shakers." Jesus says, "Blessed are the peacemakers... "

Our culture says, "Blessed are the *expedient* — the compromisers — the conformists. Blessed are those who don't rock the boat." Jesus says, "Blessed are those who are persecuted for righteousness sake... "

Our culture says, "Blessed are those who *exercise authority* — who lord it over others. Blessed are the *big wheels.*"

Jesus says, "It shall not be so among you; but whoever wants to be first among you must be your servant."

In a world turned against God, *where will you place your faith?*

## 49

**R**ighteousness is *relationship.*

All our first parents had to do to be righteous was to *have faith in God.* To be godlike they simply had to *believe and trust God.*

*God said,* "Eat not... if you do, you die!"

*The serpent said,* "You will not die — you will be like God... "

*They had to choose* to believe God...

Or to *believe the serpent.*

They *rejected God's word* — believed the serpent — rejected the truth — accepted the lie.

The *relationship with God was broken* by mistrust — and disobedience.

They were separated from God and *death is separation.*

In rejection — in disbelief of God — *they lost their perfection.*

They *sacrificed their godlikeness...* their righteousness.

Their self-alienation from God *passed on to all human progeny.*

Which is why it is *easy not to believe God!* Easy to believe a lie.

The entire Bible is a *record of God's attempt to win humans back* to Himself — to reconcile them — to redeem them.

His *supreme effort* was His Son Jesus Christ on the cross!

He offers righteousness — that is a personal relationship with Himself — through Jesus Christ... *which is to be received through faith.*

"Abraham believed God and it was credited to him as righteousness."

*— Genesis 15:6*

"This is the work of God that you believe on Him whom He has sent."

*— John 6:29*

"To as many as received Him, to those who believed on His name, He gave the right to become children of God."

*— John 1:12*

# 50

**W**hat kind of a God would *send people to hell?*

Not an uncommon question — betraying a *caricature of God* — not the reality.

The *God of the Bible* does not send anyone to hell!

On the contrary, He has done *everything in His power to keep people out of hell.*

*Which is what the life of Jesus Christ is all about!*

Faith in Jesus Christ is where eternal life is found — eternity with God.

Over the gate of hell there is *a Man on a cross...*

Jesus, the Son of God, *whom He sent to prevent people from going to hell.*

One must *ignore that man on the cross* — squeeze past Him — to get into hell!

God has done all in His power to keep us out of hell... but it would have been *immoral of God not to prepare a place for those who refused to go to heaven!*

Eternity in the city of God is for *all who desire it* — who seek it — who want it!

Hell is or those who *choose otherwise.*

One goes to hell by choice.

*His own!*

"All we like sheep have gone astray, we have turned everyone to his on way; and the Lord has laid on Him the iniquity of us all."

*— Isaiah 53:6*

"For our sake God made Him who had no sin to be sin for us, so that in Him we might become the righteousness of God."

*— II Corinthians 5:21*

"Believe on the Lord Jesus Christ, and you will be saved!"

*— Acts 16:31*

# 51

**H**uman perfection includes absolute freedom.

Freedom even to sin!

God created man perfect... *Adam and Ever were free to sin* — free to disbelieve God — to disobey God.

And they did!

By which rebellion *humanity lost its perfection...*

And *its freedom.*

Jesus Christ was perfect... that is, free to sin — *free to disbelieve His Heavenly Father and disobey Him.*

But *He chose not to!*

Thereby *retaining His perfection...*

And *His freedom!*

By His death and resurrection *all who believe will be perfected...* that is, liberated.

*Sin enslaves...* righteousness liberates.

*To be righteous is to be free...* even to sin.

To reject righteousness through faith is to be in bondage... the sinner *is not free not to sin.*

*The fundamental distinction between righteousness and sin is faith.*

*The fundamental issue in history is faith.*

God spoke in the garden — the serpent contradicted His word...

Eve had to *believe* one or the other.

*She chose the serpent...* and obeyed him.

That choice remains to this day *the fundamental choice for each of us...* and our perfection — and freedom — hang on our choice.

"By faith we understand that the universe was formed at God's command, so that what is seen was not made out of what was visible... And without faith it is impossible to please God, because anyone who comes to Him must believe that He exists and that He rewards those who earnestly seek Him."

— *Hebrews 11:3, 6*

## 52

**M**an is *incurably religious* — the religion to which most subscribe is secular humanism…

*Man's belief in himself!*

The Bible, from Genesis to Revelation, is a record of the *human failure*… even when man enjoyed human perfection fresh from the hand of the Creator.

Man's institutions, programs, and plans have *all failed*… organizations — education — legislation have failed.

He amasses knowledge and skills — achieves incredible things technologically and scientifically — and *his very achievement becomes a threat to his survival.*

Despite which *secular humanism* persists as his religion!

Ever since the serpent in his subtlety convinced our first parents in the Garden of Eden that *God* had deceived them…

By tempting them to *virtue* — to *goodness* — to *god-likeness* by their *own effort*… he persuaded them that being like God was something which they could achieve by human means… "If you eat this fruit you will be like God… "

They *put their faith in man.*

They capitulated... even though, at the moment of temptation, they *perfectly imaged God* in their humanness.

Accepting the serpent's lie, they assumed goodness, God-likeness, and virtue were *goals* to be *achieved by human effort!* They doubted the perfection of their creation... they rejected God and His word... and they believed and obeyed the serpent.

They ate the fruit... and died! They were *separated from God.*

The relationship had been broken... and to this day, *human effort for perfection* has continued to alienate man from God.

In his stubborn pride, man rejects God and struggles to perfect himself, thus *compounding his frustration* as his achievements fail to bring the fulfillment promised and threaten human survival.

Faith in man separated from God is an illusion. Man is only man, as he was meant to be, when he is *right with God*... only as he lives in dependence upon God is he truly independent and fulfilled!

"You shall have no other gods before me."

— *Exodus 20:3*

## 53

**G**od is a God of things *as they are…*
Not as *we wish they would be!*
And *He works in things as they are.*
Faith *begins at this point…*
With things *as they are…*
And a God *who is there.*
Faith that *ignores facts* misses the point.
It is *not faith* at all…
It is (at best) *wishful thinking.*
Authentic faith has a *healthy regard for the facts…*
However *difficult or negative…*
But faith rests in the *supreme fact…*
*The God of things as they are!*

Abraham knew that a son by Sarah was *an impossibility* — he was a hundred years old and Sarah was past ninety.

Besides which, *she had never been able to get pregnant.*

Abraham *did not ignore the facts...*

But *He believed God...*

And *God made the difference.* "With God all things are possible."

"By faith Abraham, even though he was past age — and Sarah herself was barren — was enabled to become a father because he considered him faithful who had made the promise."

*— Hebrews 11:11*

"Yet he did not waver through unbelief regarding the promise of God, but was strengthened in his faith and gave glory to God, being fully persuaded that God had power to do what He had promised."

*— Romans 4:20-21*

# 54

**L**ogistics.

*God is their Master!*

His delivery system is perfect…

He is able to handle any and every vicissitude or exigency…

No matter what happens, *God is able to work in it and through it* to bring to pass His perfect plan.

In His sovereign purpose *God has guaranteed human freedom and responsibility.*

And in His sovereign purpose *God works His will.*

God *will not interfere* with human freedom…

Human freedom *cannot frustrate* God's purpose.

Those who put their faith in God — trust Him — believe Him — submit to His will — *even though they may fail and sin* — enjoy the blessing of His perfect logistical system.

By the catalyst of His grace — God will *transform human weakness and error into blessing.*

God can take *the worst* that man can do... and turn it into *the best thing that could happen*.

If fact, *He has done just that* with the crucifixion of Jesus Christ.

Humanity put the *only perfect man* who ever lived on the cross...

That's the *worst evil possible*.

God turned that event into *redemption* for the whole human race...

That's the *best possible* blessing.

That's *perfection in logistics!*

Regardless of your circumstances, *put your faith in God*.

"Now faith is being sure of what we hope for and certain of what we cannot see. This is what the ancients were commended for... These were all commended for their faith, yet none of them received what had been promised. God had planned something better for us so that only together with us would they be made perfect."

— *Hebrews 11:1, 39-40*

**P**eople are hopeless because *they hope in the wrong things!*

They cast about for something on which to pin their hopes — then suffer when it fails. *Having no trustworthy foundation*, hope becomes nothing more than wishful thinking.

Basically *the problem is one of hoping in that which is visible* — tangible — material... about which the Bible is very explicit: "That which is seen is temporal — that which is unseen is eternal."

Obviously, *hope in the temporary is doomed!*

How fragile is *hope in hope-so things*: real estate — silver and gold — stocks and bonds — position — power — prestige — popularity.

When such hope fails it leaves *frustration* — brokenness — unmitigated regret — failure... often suicide.

Success is often worse because it *turns out to be something else than was hoped for* — loneliness — emptiness — meaninglessness — alcoholism — divorce — heart attacks... often suicide.

Nothing could be worse than *hope that is hopeless!*

In the Bible *hope is a noun* — not a verb. It is something we possess — not something we do. It is the gift of God — not a self-generated optimism, grasping at straws.

God has given the human family a hope which is the fulfillment of *everything the human heart longs for* — justice — peace — freedom — human rights — no sorrow — no tears — no pain — no war — no death.

God promises all that — an infinitely more — *a reality that transcends human language to verbalize.*

His guarantee is Jesus Christ! Jesus' entry into history is the *earnest of all that God promises* those whose hope is in Him.

As the Old Testament predicted thousands of details which were fulfilled in Christ — so the New Testament presents a *clear picture of the consummation of history* and the perfection of the divine economy.

His "plan for the fullness of time, to unite all things in Christ."

— *Ephesians 1:10*

Hope in Jesus Christ is certain hope which cannot fail!

## 56

**A** Christian leader is one who knows where he is going."
Sounds great... but *is it true?*
It was said of Abraham, *father of faith:* "He went out, not knowing where he was to go." (Hebrews 11:8)

A dramatic contrast which illustrates the fundamental distinction between contemporary evangelical thinking and biblical thinking.

"For my thoughts are not your thoughts, neither are your ways my ways," declares the Lord. "As the heavens are higher than the earth, so are my ways higher than your ways and my thoughts higher than your thoughts."

*— Isaiah 55:8-9*

Here are the *marks of the way of faith* — the pilgrimage with Christ...

"By faith Abraham, when called to go to a place... obeyed and went, even though he did not know where he was going. By faith he made his home in the promised land like a stranger in a foreign country."

*— Hebrews 11:8-9*

"By faith Noah... in holy fear built an ark to save his family. By his faith he condemned the world and became heir of the righteousness that comes by faith."

*— Hebrews 11:7*

"By faith Moses... chose to be mistreated along with the people of God rather than to enjoy the pleasure of sin for a short time. He regarded disgrace for the sake of Christ as of greater value than the treasures of Egypt, not fearing the king's anger."

*— Hebrews 11:24-26*

Paul believed "that which is seen is temporal. That which is not seen is eternal."

*— II Corinthians 4:18*

The tragedy of contemporary ideas of faith is that failure to get results indicates *they have too little faith.*

We need to be liberated from *bondage to the visible,* the quantifiable, the temporal. We need to learn to "walk by faith, not by sight!"

"And what more shall I say? I do not have time to tell about Gideon, Barak, Samson, Jephthah, David, Samuel and the prophets, who through faith conquered kingdoms... These were all commended for their faith, yet none of them received what had been promised. God had planned something better... "

*— Hebrews 11:32-33, 39-40*

## 57

The hurrier I go... the behinder I get."

The plight of the man who lets enthusiasm victimize him.

He doesn't possess zeal... *zeal possesses him!*

Mistaking hysteria for urgency, a man may run off in all directions at once... his *energy and effort so diffused* that its force is spent long before a purpose is achieved...

Like hitting a target with a head of cabbage.

Acting in haste — without taking time to let his zeal soak in prayer and counsel — his projects peter out... *abortive because premature!*

Without the seasoning, maturing process of *prayerful reflection*, ideas — no matter how good — generally lack the strength of fulfillment.

Patience is more than a human virtue... it is the Spirit of God — and it is the essence of great Christian faith.

Have faith in God... and wait!

*Let the idea spawn...* it will produce offspring.

Heed the counsel of one of the most profound devotional writers. He knew the "mind of Christ" and speaks out of *deep, seasoned, tempered wisdom.*

"Never act in a panic, nor allow man to dictate to thee. Calm thyself and be still. Force thyself into the quiet of thy closet until thy pulse beats normally and the scare has ceased to disturb."

"When thou are most eager to act is the time when thou wilt make the *most pitiable mistakes.*"

"Do not say in thine heart what thou wilt or wilt not do, but wait upon thy God *until He makes known His way.*"

"So long as that way is hidden, it is clear that there is no need of action… and that *He accounts Himself responsible* for all the result of keeping thee where thou are."

— *F.B. Meyer*

"A simple man believes anything, but a prudent man gives thought to his steps."

— *Proverbs 14:15*

## 58

**H**igh and dry."

Dry because high…

That's the status of the proud one…

High and dry.

High in ego — *low in spirituality.*

High in pride — *low in moral courage and integrity.*

High in self-righteousness — *shriveled up in soul and spirit.*

Sometimes when we experience plenty we forget to put our faith in God — the One who provided us with plenty.

Jesus said, "Blessed are the poor in spirit, for theirs is the kingdom of heaven."

Symptoms of lukewarmness in the Laodicean church was precisely this — "high and dry." "You say, 'I am rich; I have acquired wealth and do not need a thing.' But you do not realize that you are wretched, pitiful, poor, blind, and naked."

— *Revelation 3:17*

Need nothing? That's the *abyss of faith.*

That is salt which has lost its savor.

As Jesus was unable to help the proud Pharisee impressed with his own piety, so *Jesus can help no one who needs nothing.*

In the most basic sense *Christ came for failures!*

There is *no limit to what He can do* for the one who humbles himself and asks for grace.

But that requires *transferring our faith from ourselves to our God.*

The mighty apostle Paul understood this: "My strength is made perfect in weakness... therefore I take pleasure in my infirmities... because when I am weak, then am I strong."

*— II Corinthians 12:10*

Begin low with Christ... and the sky's the limit!

"For whoever exalts himself shall be humbled, and whoever humbles himself shall be exalted."

*— Matthew 23:12*

"God resists the proud and gives grace to the humble."

*— I Peter 5:5*

## 59

The *irresistible future...*

Or the present *as good as we can make it?*

*Worthy of contemplation.*

The future is irresistible — not just because it is inevitable — but because *it feeds our hope.*

Expectation for the future is the *strongest motivation* in the present.

The student *studies hard* in grade school to make Junior High — in Junior High to make High School — in High School to make college — in college to earn the degree...

Graduate school perhaps — because of the *promise implicit* in an advanced degree.

Beyond the degree is a *career — marriage — home — family...*

Then *work hard to succeed* — save — retire...

The future *keeps compelling us on.*

But what *after retirement?*

After the travel — the leisure — the *fulfilling of dreams hoped for in the early years...*

*No future?*

And what of those *whom age has laid aside* — the elderly in a nursing home — the helpless — the dependent...

No future? *No hope?*

The Christian always has hope — because we have *put our faith in God!*

"Do not let your hearts be troubled. Trust in God, trust also in me. In my Father's house are many rooms; if it were not so, I would have told you. I am going there to prepare a place for you. And if I go and prepare a place for you, I will come back and take you to be with me that you also may be where I am."

— *John 14:1-3*

## 60

**I**n the final analysis, *you've got to put your faith in somebody…*

Even if that somebody is yourself alone.

*Some kind of faith* is inescapable.

Either you believe in God or you believe in yourself.

If you believe in God, either you believe in the God of the Bible or some other…

If you believe in some other god, then you believe that the Bible is untrustworthy.

If you believe the Bible is untrustworthy, *you must have some basis* for such a belief. What is it? Who or what do you believe strongly enough to allow you to put aside the Scripture?

Will the foundation of your belief stand *the test of reality?*

The *eternal welfare of your soul* rides on this!

Either you trust Jesus Christ — His Word and His Work — or you do not.

If you do not, *on whom or what rests your eternal destiny?*

Perhaps you do not believe in immortality. Very well, *what is the foundation*

*for this belief?* Where did you get it? Is your source trustworthy? Is it intelligent to risk your future with this source?

Is the foundation of your belief *reliable enough* to justify your rejection of Jesus Christ and His gift of eternal life?

If the basis of your "faith" against Jesus and immortality is rational... is it *dependable?*

To put it another way, *do you have a reasonable faith* — or just opinions?

Assuming there is a risk in believing the Bible, in trusting Jesus Christ — is there a lesser risk in your belief? *Where does the greater risk lie...* in trusting Jesus, or something else — or someone else?

What person in history more merits your confidence? Who else than Jesus has so *earned the right* to be trusted by you?

You have a faith! Is it based on fact... or fancy?

"Blessed are those who hear the word of God and obey it."

— *Luke 11:28*

"Have faith in God!"

— *Mark 11:22*